JUDGMENT

JUDGMENT
STANDING ON A PLAIN

ARIEL

TATE PUBLISHING
AND ENTERPRISES, LLC

Published by Tate Publishing & Enterprises, LLC
127 E. Trade Center Terrace | Mustang, Oklahoma 73064 USA
1.888.361.9473 | www.tatepublishing.com

Tate Publishing is committed to excellence in the publishing industry. The company reflects the philosophy established by the founders, based on Psalm 68:11,
"The Lord gave the word and great was the company of those who published it."

Book design copyright © 2016 by Tate Publishing, LLC. All rights reserved.
Cover design by Norlan Balazo
Interior design by Gram Telen

Published in the United States of America

ISBN: 978-1-68254-535-5
1. Religion / Essays
2. Religion / Biblical Commentary / General
15.10.29

Contents

Preface

The following statements may not be easily accepted by mankind because to the men and women of this generation and generations past, if what is being presented is not something they came up with themselves, or want, or if they do not agree with it, or their experts cannot confirm it, then they will deem it as not being true or relevant in their opinion, so they will go on without understanding the portent until too late, as many before them already have done.

—Ariel

The Summons to All
in the
Trial and Judgment of Man

Come, let us reason together

Mankind stands on a plain.

Judgment (the trial of Man and Satan)

…just not the way it was expected to come about.

I am Ariel incarnate; I stand now as prosecutor of mankind and of Satan, and this is the beginning of the end.

To those who have fallen asleep, now waking up:

Was it not stated there would be the event; you would not know the day or the hour it would come upon you; and the event, one of accountability—judgment? In that the event could not be foretold, *is evidence the end of prophecy has come with it*; it has come, is passing, and in passing, signifying further the beginning of the end to all things.

Be assured, this is not simply speculation or hearsay presented, nor the staging of a mock trial in preparation for some future event as will be proven within this writing and hereafter. The evidence, as is described here, is *Revelation's* small book, and *is* the actual determination of the judgment of humanity and of Satan, for all past and present questionable acts men inflict upon other humans and upon themselves.

As for men, countless have dedicated their lives to their religions, ideologies, and prophecies thereof, many leading and misleading. Other men promise solutions and relief to the world; others, through their distractions, blanket the world in misperceptions. The constant redirection of all which might be considered valuable holds the unwary in a state of perpetual competition, exhaustion, and distress. The world's population, both past and present—unsatisfied time and time again—has risen up, and rises up in turbulence to crush, or falls into a stupor. It is the *sea* of humanity in the throes of sin of which I speak, and the imminent destruction thereof.

As you will come to understand through this writing, during this event, it makes no difference where you physically view yourself as standing; you will see how it is that man, past, present, and future, *is* simultaneously standing as visible before the court and before God as the *sea of humanity. Man, created in God's image, is more than the creature he perceives himself to be.*

Prologue to Prosecution

Man has had thousands of years of upheaval, rebellion, and questionable existence; and in the course of that time, mankind's Creator warned mankind: it could not and would not continue; giving mankind an option to choose a different course of action, before it came to the point where God would intervene and bring those things to an end. It is understood: *man, in response, has made his own determination and case*, to ignore the documented statements and warnings as evident through the choices made (and being made) in conducting ongoing affairs; all of which continue to be well documented as well as revered so as to be taught in man's institutes of learning.

So as it stands, men in every manner and pursuit, present themselves as authorities to other men, presenting their cases and actions daily through the words they wield. The prosecution presents this case of judgment against Humanity and Satan, in the spirit of the truth, of the words being submitted here before God, the court, the witnesses, and all humanity.

The court sits.

The prosecution now takes the lead in detailing testimony and actions of these proceedings, detailing the charges and evidence against mankind and Satan to all who exist—past, present, and future—through this writing.

This prosecutor presents to the court the following: list of Humanity's offenses; opening statement; evidence of Humanity's origin and composition; evidence of and the offenses; clarification of the sentence of those found responsible for committing and perpetuating the offenses of mankind; the prosecution's decree.

The prosecution's description of the list of Humanity's offenses:

> The denial of accountability to God.
> The denial of the truth of origin and essence.
> The denial of accountability to one another.
> The denial of the spirit of truth in daily life.
> The denial of the word of God in the means to change.

Opening Statement: to God, the Court, the Witnesses, and the Whole of Humanity

It is without question: mankind is a species unto himself. However, it is not enough upon which to base justification for mankind to just continue as they have in the multitude of offenses which compromise and scar the lives of children; children who grow up to be similar examples, compromising and scarring another generation of children after them; and so the spirit wanes. And if the spirit wanes, there is justification to bring the waning of the spirit of the species called man, to an end.

In the knowledge of all who have existed, do exist, and may come to exist, *is* not being a child a commonality of mankind? A plain and simple truth upon which everyone stands their entire life, *in that they will always have been a child to someone*; and in this knowledge is it not truth that every child should be carefully, honorably, diligently, justly watched over at every stage of their life, even if a child's parents are not there to do it themselves? Is this not a sign of an intelligent reasoning culture?

Providing justly for the species is what man says he is doing throughout most daily activities; however, there is ample evidence this has not been, and is not the case. Not all are being provided for equitably, and what is being provided is filled with or tainted with corruption. Man's real motivations for his actions, and the subsequent rewards received for the activities, reveals man as having a different nature; one in contradiction to Godly precepts. The manner in which man defines understandings and arrives at his justifications are in part the issues at hand.

The plain truth of commonality, of simply being children (children requiring loving care and guidance), *is* the same plain of reasoning (area, ground, level, plane, structure, premise, foundation—Armageddon, Megiddo, Way of the Sea, A Place of Crowds) upon which every man, woman, and child has warred and is warring with one another, saying in your hearts and through your actions, *It shall not be you and your child. I will prevail and, by my ideology and striving, dig my trenches around me, build up my fortress (security) and my future. And it will be me and my offspring and those I designate, who shall be secure, comforted, and entitled.* Man is created in the image of a caring, honorable, devoted, just God. These unceasing, selfish, and heartless wars should have never existed for a reasoning species. There has always been a different path upon which to walk.

Through the means of irrefutable truths, comparative evidence, documents authored by God and men, the prosecution will prove the actions of mankind as offenses to the concept of life of the species; thus proving the need to impose and execute a level of justice upon humanity, whatever it may take, such as to resolve for all time the offenses of humanity, such that the offenders and the acts they commit never again be remembered, let alone be permitted to continue.

Evidence of Humanity's Origin and Composition

The more recent pursuits of man have come to be a significant source of distraction, preventing man from focusing on key pieces of evidence of the actual functioning of society (man), from grasping the larger picture of his existence.

What man has overlooked deliberately, or in being unconscientiously shortsighted, yet the court has witnessed: Thousands of years ago, mankind understood and wrote about concepts and things he could not physically discern with the eyes—deity, philosophy, ideology, abstracts, invisibility, morality, even presenting tales of mythological gods, well before he could begin to understand the things around him enough to exploit them, even before beginning to understand the functioning and details of his very own body. The knowledge of the sequence of these events, and the things since uncovered by men, are recorded and can be viewed in the (larger picture) details of God's Word and man's books.

This is to say: *Man long ago understood* (valued, made determination of) what is considered as not discernable to the eye, *well before he could understand the images of those components the eyes took in*, such as in the relatively recent discovery of the evolution of the world around him, leading him into the industrial era, into the present era of excess and exploitation.

This was no accident that mankind in the beginning contemplated on a different plane than the other species: discerning aspects and probabilities of the heavens, possessing knowledge of right and wrong, *even while existing in a perceived primitive state*, so as to perform acts of respect and reverence. Acts of reverence, while skewed by the sins (spirits) of bias and doubt, still served man for a time, preventing mankind from spiritually venturing far away from the Creator, until today; until the fullness of the Gentiles.

Therefore, it is proven here, there is no excuse for leaders who have been educated throughout the generations with such knowledge, whose educated predecessors of bygone civilizations documented the philosophies and accounts in historic writings, to say, "I didn't know" or that "God does not exist."

The leaders of men, avoid bringing such obvious insights to the attention of the rest of mankind through educational branches, because to do so would mean the leaders would have to acknowledge the Creator and the Creator's precepts; and in doing such, give up their explorations, justifications, ideologies, positions, powers, and entitlements. And because of these things, both leaders and followers have come to allow themselves the opportunity to explore every pursuit without regard or consideration as to the consequences of doing so.

The Understanding of the Invisible God and Man Created in His image; the Invisible Man

If what has just been presented not enough to acknowledge truth and the actual order of things, there is the composition and functioning of mankind, and in this instance, an understanding through the evidence of the functioning of the eye.

In their studies, lost in ignorance, or having disregard of the truth of man's historical beginnings, scientists and medical experts delve deeper and deeper into the makeup of man, *looking* with their eyes, *for a physical explanation for reasoning and intellect*; and in doing so, miss, or ignore, or deliberately obscure, a very obvious truth concerning the eye, leading others to be so misled.

Man cannot see anything with the eye; Man can only reason any matter: "Come, let us reason together."

Read Genesis 3:7. Before man sinned, he solely reasoned matters from the soul and not from what his eyes told him. When man sinned, his eyes (perceptions) were opened to recognize he was naked; thereafter, his awareness came more and more to be attached to the components of the physical dimension, as it is today.

Today, as it has come to be more recognized by the specialists (and yet, has always been), *the eye does not have a mind, nor does the mind have an eye.*

What the learned scientist, medical, philosophical, metaphysical, educational, and other experts do not say, is that no matter how far into any aspect of the physical dimension man goes, *what man determines through the functioning of the eye will* never *actually be seen.* Observe the synonyms for "seen"—observed, perceived, distinguished, noticed, witnessed, spotted, glimpsed, made out (i.e., *reasoned*). To "see" or having "seen" denotes an essence doing the seeing *as having intellect with the ability to reason or understand on it's own basis of composition.* But as is understood, the eye does not have a mind.

To imply the eye has "seen" something, based on the synonyms described above, *implies the eye as having a power to somehow reason the image* in such a way so as to make the image, and any aspect or value of the image composite, in an active way discernable to the mind; however, it is only an eye. You open the eye and whatever photons (image) happen to be around enter the eye; the photons (image) are automatically flipped upside down; the photons (image) are automatically absorbed and processed through an automatic functioning of the cones and rods. And that is the end of the photons (image). Matters, *both physical and spiritual*, are only reasoned (assigned value) elsewhere within the composite called man, i.e., there is no power in the eye to provide an understanding of a matter, nor assign a value nor discern a value.

While the specialists put it into words of their own (branch of) understanding, *removing you from perceiving the simplicity of the actual function*, what you are identifying as images of things outside your body are, in truth, nothing more than a neurological reconstruction in the mind; an integrated construct consisting of patterns of particle energy flow, analyzed and instantaneously reasoned by the soul in the spirit of truth; each and every object a single, or composite, of *spiritually reasoned* concepts having a variety of values operating and functioning, simultaneously reasoned, *expressed in terms of words.*

In the least and greatest sense, it is therefore proven historically, and even to this day, no man can say they see or have seen with their eyes, another physical man; it can only be said a man reasons (or reasoned) the conceptual "physical" aspects of other men. *This makes man as invisible to one another, and everything else on the physical plane as functionally and conceptually invisible; and man a far different creature than man presently understands himself to be.*

Upon this plain truth of understanding (truthful foundation), with man's existence as being only the reasoning of one another, *is the functional conceptual place where God sees (reasons, understands) man as being children of God*, even if any man chooses not to reason (see) God.

Man, reasoning only physical elements and spiritual abstracts, not knowing his own physical makeup until more recently, did not and could not have possessed the reasoning to invent himself with reason before understanding his own physical composition. The connection to the Father is undeniable.

Man uniquely exists in two dimensions. A person conducts the act of reasoning aspects of the *physical dimension* only through the consciousness (soul), recognizing, assessing, and assigning value to any concept which happens as coming through their five senses.

When choosing to do so, the soul may also enter into a state (area, level, plane) so as to focus only on levels of the *spiritual dimension*, also making assessments and assignment of value to any number of abstracts realized within their own consciousness, such as compassion, dedication, joy, love, respect, consideration, creativity, generosity, caring, et al., one by one or combined. This is the functioning of the "man" created in the image of the to be reasoned only invisible God. (God exists as specific abstract concepts and words, each word having a value that complements one another so as to culminate as a whole entity with specific definitions, and there is only one such Being. Adding the words of the concept of having been created by God and consigned to exist in the flesh (physical dimension) for a time, Man is to attain *to the reasoning* of the same specific complimentary abstract words and concepts to which has been assigned to him in being created in God's image—and none other.)

That which is to be reasoned. Breakdown any given composition or concept, abstract or physical, and describe it. It is nothing more than words *for the purpose of reasoning… for any purpose.*

Recall it was said, "The waters were separated." But it was not said that an *entity* could not traverse or transfigure from one dimension to another. God and man, the heavens and earth, through God's understanding, consists only of the "words" of the composition of the particular dimension; as in the composite "God's Word" as capable of existing in both dimensions, and "flesh-eating virus" which is only as existing in the physical dimension. As man *is* created in God's image, man can traverse through reasoning from one level to another.

God, a purely spiritual entity, gave no portion of Himself "likeness-of-man" physical words of composition (a body consisting of flesh, DNA, hair, spleen, blood, et al.), *until it became necessary to reach man on a level where man perceived himself at the time;* a level where man had compromised himself to the extent so as to only understand himself on the physical level, only reasoning (seeing) and relating to the pursuits of the flesh (eyes); a place also where the generation, and generations to come, were perceived to be without awareness, direction, hope, or a future, as it is again today.

God's understanding of the value of words. The power of the soul's consciousness brings words together to provide an understanding of the likenesses (images) of what exists outside the body, in order for the soul, while in the body for a short time, to have the ability to function *within* the word-based parameters of the physical world. Yet, beyond these things, lay the abstracts which reason the whole together.

Describe anything, you do so in words; and words are only reasoned and not by the eye. The specialists will explain every detail of their perception of the physical components in their words and bring you no closer to understanding than the words they use, the words of the physical dimension.

With what has just been stated, did, does, or will God ever expect you to know every minute detail of anything physical, as does the alleged experts expect, or did God simply expect that the species called man conduct themselves respectfully?

Men survived with far less knowledge of their surroundings than what is known today, and what has come to be uncovered has not resolved one social issue, only succeeding in complicating man's understanding of man. The spiritual-reasoning man who co-existed with God in the Garden, did not know and had no need to know, the detailed functioning of the brain nor the workings of any physical element; yet the leaders throughout man's existence, supported by the testimonies and discoveries of their witnesses (experts), promote the necessity of understanding things as they do, as the priorities upon which the world is to focus.

Once innately connected to God through far fewer words (such as trust, devotion, dedication, diligence, likeness, care, respect), man, sent out into the world because of his disobedience, in revolt, has come to *more value* the images (and sounds) of those things which exist outside his body, treating the photon images received by the eye, (and the vibrating air molecules upon the ear mechanism) as if they are the means to solve the problems of the world. So most every possibility uncovered, or most every scenario imagined, is explored, discussed, and proclaimed the (possible) truth, except for the reasonable obvious.

Man lost spiritual sight in the realization there is "more" substance and more value within the "abstract word" constructs of his soul (consciousness) as in the case of the words "ability to determine an actual value of a concept to humanity" in the process, steering himself away from the reality (and understanding) of having a Creator who may not reveal himself often, yet who is still watching (seeing, reasoning).

The "more" being the connection and access into the heavens is the dimension which co-exists, but separately with the physical dimension as has been described in God's

Word. In being created in God's image, God's Word has been, and is, man's direct connection (a conduit) to God the Father. Were the visions of the prophets: the heavens, and of cherubim, seraphim, angels, created only for the scriptures?

As man *is* created in God's reasoning image, *a heavenly creature in his own right*, every man intuitively knows heavenly entities exist in a realm of understandings long since ignored, or forgotten, or obscured by physical concepts which man has chosen to value over reasoning. It should come to man's attention that the responsibilities of the (invisible to the eye) heavenly entities and the (invisible to the eye) army, have not changed, and as eternal creatures existing on an invisible-to-the-eye reasoning level, which co-exists with the physical plane, they are the witnesses to *every action* of the downfall of man, each and every day.

Having been created in God's image (words), with every possibility readily available, the soul of a child need simply have been told, in the spirit of truth, what words are to be recognized and valued—"raise up a *child* in the way they should go…their entire life." (Notice this does not say raise up an "adult".)

Having *not* been raised up in the way they should go, there are many who, misguided through guilt, through real or imagined anger, through ignorance, are putting themselves through, or are being forced by alleged specialists, into an endless series of speculations and possibilities to solve their problems, these processes being designed by those wanting and needing recognition of their worldly expertise and authority. Those who are also coveting the power and entitlements bestowed upon them for their misdirection and perceived understandings.

In the case of the religious, pieties, platitudes, and supplications fill the air; these are the actions of men devoid of actual understanding of their own construct, and of how they are created in God's image and where everything stands as visible or invisible, or they would be standing as different examples to each other and to the generations to come.

Men appear as examples to one another, to God, to this court, and to the witnesses, as having no regard or consideration for altering his state of sin and existing perceptions to consider what manner entity he has been created to be and is; and from all indications, values only everything his five (5) senses tell him; disregarding the wisdom of the spirit for the abstracts such as in the "need to be cautious," opting for or settling for other abstracts: complacency, diversions, rituals, recognition, exploitation, instant gratification, excess, and entitlements.

Man has existed and exists within a specific set of standards and principles of his own desire, of his own individual making. A state of existence which he created for himself to justify compromised actions and lack of accountability, allowing himself the opportunity to turn, to revel in every possibility, and exploit the branches of studies stemming from the *whole of knowledge*; a compilation of every possibility—symbolized in the concept of the Tree of the Knowledge of Good and Evil. And in doing so, man perpetuates false hope to the generations to come, even conversely renewing doubts daily; *having been bit (seduced) by a serpent's understanding of matters* as was Adam and Eve; poisoned and poisoning others with every new morsel discovered, consumed, and shared from the tree called Abyss.

Man, was cast out of *a state of consciousness (awareness) defined as a garden*. Is not a garden created for the purposes of tranquility, pleasure, peacefulness, serenity, comfort, inspiration, delight, generosity, relaxation, joy, invigoration, diversity, cultivation, perpetuity, et al.?

In sin, man's eyes were opened and turned outward into the world; the "invisible to the eye" proverbial garden had been cut off from man's reasoning perceptions. Man had disobeyed; man had only the obligation to humble himself to the concept of "obedience" in order to seek out and find the *conceptual tree of life* which goes by the name Equity (look at the synonyms), which for mankind exists within the boundaries of (and covers as having a canopy over) the aforementioned plain truth of commonality of "childhood." *Man is a child at all times: to God the Father, creator of his soul, and to his parents, creators of his flesh*. Because man believes he sees with his eyes and desires only what he can see, this tree called Equity stands as invisible to the heart of his understanding.

Equity was to be spiritually consumed (reasoned) for the healing concepts which are found as attached truths stemming from the far fewer number of specific branches of studies. Seek and ye shall find…has man yet even desired to seek out and find a tree (a sheltering concept structure which can provide every spiritually life-sustaining component man needs to spiritually survive) which exists so as to provide wisdom and contentment? Man appears to look for nothing, unless it can be exploited for selfish gain, as in promoting the branches of "economy" so as to continue to put wealth into the hands of the entitled and the tyrannical, as is seen from the heavens and the earth.

As man denies understanding of God, he therefore denies understanding (and value) of his actual self. And so as it is, the documented statements (mantras, slogans, creeds, rules, declarations, proclamations, profit statements, constitutions, educational pursuits, et al.) written by men, and passed around for all to read and follow, are written with the blood (lifeblood, i.e., life) of men as the ink; belying (proving false) man's search for truth and equity for the species. And so deceptions continue, despite the obvious.

The relevance of the abstract concept of "value" is undeniable. As understood in the actions of Adam and Eve, who contemplated (reasoned) over the value of something physical over the value of obedience, many have been foolishly seduced to be drawn out into the physical world around them, continuously looking for value after value of the physical world.

And as in the case of prophecy, many have been *looking* for signs you can see with your eyes as to when the event was to take place, when you can't "see" things to begin with.

And as it has been stated, even if it were signs as occurring outside the body, it would only still be a neurological reconstruction within your consciousness—matters to be reasoned spiritually. Being faithful and obedient to be guided by a Trinity designated to provide man with the power (God's power—"know yet not that you are the temple of the Lord?") of truthful (Spirit of Truth—"I will send you the Comforter who will guide you in all things") understanding (God's Word—"Lo, I am with you always").

How many teach by *example* this nearness of God, let alone comprehend the implications? So it is when the religious teach, they teach their own values (mind). Every externally definable ritual they can think of, that might be slightly the same or totally different than the next religion's, makes them stand out *not* as being of the same mind, but of being the same ilk; intent on promoting themselves for the position of separation and entitlements thereof. There are no such separations between men entering into, and those within, the kingdom of God.

When man, created in God's image, allowed himself to become self-absorbed, seduced and distracted by earthly matters, he lost discernment and value, literally and figuratively, of his unique spiritual nature and character; demeaning and abasing himself, trying to and succeeding in *proving* himself as unworthy; continually seeking his own solutions in order to make things right; not recognizing he can never be separated from God.

What learned and God-fearing leader of any sort has bothered to herald daily the following: Just as the undoing of man, has been through the temptation of Satan; man has always had the opportunity to be the undoing of Satan, by refusing to be corrupted by the temptations in the world. What a comeback or overcoming for man that would be; to bring down the evil in the heavens and the world.

God revealed His desire for mankind to make the choice to return to God which would remove Satan's power in man's life, in the scripture "God seeks what has passed." What had "passed" was the relationship once had between man and God in the both figuratively and literally invisible garden. The stated scripture "God seeks what has passed" implies God as waiting (for a time) for the event to occur, which also *implies man as having been given the power* to return, effect change, and bring down Satan. And yet, did the religious make this case known to the leaders? And where can one find a man who has cast aside the (desire, and perceptions of the) world to make a complete return to God?

In the directive "Be ye perfect as your Father in heaven is perfect," which words of this understanding does man live by; were the words not to be God's Word?

God has spoken of a change and offered the only solution possible to resolve what man had carelessly discarded—a way to understand himself—as perfect *forgiveness*. Acknowledging his connection to the Father, which *is* the only means for man to conquer Satan, elevating man above the stature of being Satan's mindless minion.

(What is man?) Man had been given and has had ample time, thousands of years, to consider all possibilities.

So while each and every one have been seduced, only reasoning and seeking understanding through *expanding the idea of yourselves through so many worldly achievements,* through exploitation of every pursuit in the physical world around you, looking for the answers outside of yourselves; reveling in every distraction; corrupting and perpetuating corruption, in the soul, body, and the world; your intentions and actions are and have been followed, and are judged, not through anything physical as in the construction of the body or the elements in the world. Only through the mechanism of pure truth, and of the reasoning of being internally and eternally connected to the spiritual dimension through the power of reasoning. And you have cut yourself off and not returned.

Evidence of, and the Offenses

As God, the court, mankind, and witnesses understand, an action cannot be conceived unless there are the abstract concepts known as "motivation" and "desire" to do so.

First, from all which could possibly exist in the physical world, man (even having think-tanks upon which to consider his future, and having all manner of experts in the study of man's behavior), in having the knowledge a child has no voice so as to present their case, cares not to consider what it means to be a child in a world where the previous generations of children continuously act out selfish childish behaviors such that the conditions which existed thousands of years ago, still exist today. Where do the generations get their ideas, if it is not from the examples of leadership on multiple levels, leaders or parents, now or from the examples which came before them?

Every man and woman started from the beginning as a child, reaching out mostly playing unconditionally with one another, accepting, sharing vessels of trust. And then that child began to imitate their parents and entered a more structured environment—into the heinous dichotomy of formal education and/or into the harshness of on-the-street education. (*Dichotomy*–"a separation into two divisions that differ widely from or contradict each other" [Encarta Dictionary].)

Observe formal education: Educated men (leaders of men) have established and promote educational institutes which teach in the areas of service to humanity industries (such as in the areas of health, basic life awareness and skills, mechanics, education), and provides educational methodology so as to promote conservation of natural resources, peace, awareness; *and yet at the same time* educated men have established and promote educational institutes which teach in the areas strategies of defense and the means to build walls of security against one another, strategies of competition in every manner of institution and war, and building of financial products which promote class distinctions. And mankind's leaders continue to support and service industries whose existence relies upon exploitation of resources regardless of the cost to the whole of humanity—present and future.

Teach everything and hope it works out? With such a self-defeating system in place, can there be peace for any culture, when at the basis of daily life, everything is taught and there is only conflict between the two? Where at the end of the day all that can be said of society is that one group continues to be dissatisfied and continues to want what the other has, or they just want to do away with the other group altogether, so they can do whatever they want without restrictions? *Is this not itself, a beast, as coming up from an abyss of all knowledge from which those who desire to serve humanity cannot escape and must serve?* There are many such conceptual creatures and other abominations, erected by and towering above men, such that man serves those matters rather than serving the truth.

While these things play out, consumerism in the hands of capitalists, and through the ways of advertising (a snake in the hands of charmers), support a monetary incentive/ reward system, which puts all actual work in the hands of a few, while more and more of mankind seeks the "good life" of money parlaying and management, and careers without manual labor they have erroneously come to think as demeaning, belittling, as did and do their parents. From these things, every element, composite, concept, or reasoning, becomes property of those proclaiming it their choosing. And pieces of paper are exchanged, and entitlements are given.

This continues to escape the attention of those so wrapped in pride and in the darkness of these pursuits. No other species, existing for a day, or for hundreds of thousands of years or longer, having far less cognitive awareness or intellect, has ever had the need for a monetary incentive reward system in order to develop a symbiotic cohesive relationship with each other, and look at the exotic qualities they managed to acquire in the process.

Those species became what they are, operating under conceptual abstract life premises; words like "survival instinct" and "nurture", yet these same creatures could never and will never understand it as abstract words of their existence nor comprehend (see) those words as man does. And yet, even in having the understanding of the two simple concepts survival instinct and nurture and far more, what has man done in choosing and finalizing the words in which he is to live by? Man seeks to put men into tin cans to explore and corrupt distant worlds for profit, not bothering to see the existing devastation left behind. Man, even with the intellect to reason matters, envisioning telekinesis, levitation, astral projection, clairvoyance, does not possess the wherewithal to consider what he is; only selfishly considers what he can gather and hold onto, so nobody can take it away.

Behold the works of men, achievements, and awards. Where can one look and not see the preponderance of corruption, sloth, excess, and abuse.

No absolute accountability is necessary where there is always the delegation of authority. And the unaware, mindless, dead to everything righteous, take up the slack for mistakes made where the leaders themselves will not. You don't have to fix a problem; just find your own niche in the long line of people assigned to fix the condition.

With every conceivable resource at their fingertips, no social issues have been resolved in the thousands of years the leaders have been conducting themselves supposedly in your best interest, with every man continually supporting the forms of government and leaders, accomplishing nothing except to promote their own ideology of their entitlements.

For centuries, your leaders talk to men who only have the same objective your leaders do, the power they have, and all that comes with it. They say of the concerns: "I will take it under advisement and consult the experts and learned colleagues." And all they do when they are together is to talk in such a way, which in translation, amounts to "how to keep their power" and not about actually resolving an issue which plagues humanity. Because if the leaders solved a problem, where then could the leaders justify their position of power and entitlements (security) if they were no longer needed because they solved the problems? Instead of first presenting a solution to their peers for their approval, which leader has committed their life to resolving even one social woe with a vengeance so as to eliminate it from existence? Are they not the leaders instead of the peers? Your leaders and their peers value power more than integrity, and so it *is*, so do you. In endorsing a leader, you endorse everything they stand for.

There is another concept floating about the sea of humanity, with men waiting for their ships to come it: that which is thought of as being important called "finding people jobs." Why is it *not* noticed, that the people finding other people support jobs, themselves are the business and government leaders, having what might be considered obscene power, wealth, and entitlements—wealth from finding the means to exploit anything from the jobs which are created. Yet these same delegate most everything and/

or have others gather the words they need to make their decisions. If all that were evil were removed from the earth, then all men could work less than half of what they presently do, and it would be honest.

Associating perceived education with wealth and wealth with education, men have come to value wealth to the point where it is thought only the wealthy have the education to accomplish anything. And so they are given more wealth and power to keep things going. Does it take rewarding someone beyond comprehension, in order to get something done? Cannot integrity accomplish much?

Supported by the lies of those whom it serves, there is the lie the existing system is the best there is. There are vague promises that things will get better, but they can't. It is a system having roots in a dark and ugly past, refined and refined again, to only look more enticing to those caught up in its ways.

With the concept of delegation of authority, there is no loss of entitlements when you don't solve an adverse condition of society; it always becomes the inefficiency of the system. In the existing system, the money becomes spread way too thin, to the point where more is spent on people working on the problem, than on the problem itself, proving the monetary system doesn't solve anything. Look at the long line of institutes and organization supposedly resolving problems. And are those problems resolved? There are other means to solve conditions, but none offer up their entitlements or devious ways in exchange for them.

The way of capitalism and entertainment in the hands of the wealthy. When the self-proclaimed elite and entitled of mankind (who, coming forth as coming with power of the education system), identifies someone coming along as having a particular talent which promotes their own objectives, or knowledge that might interfere with their own objectives, they just welcome that person into the folds of the elite, and reward them recognition, exorbitant wealth, and prestige; and send them around to the other elite and entitled, to amuse them with their knowledge, and entertain them with their particular talent. These are those who care nothing about the lives of those less noticeable. Why would they, when they have such distractions and entertainment to amuse them?

Those as unaware of the pitfalls of the seduction are captured by the thought of being entitled, being envious of those welcomed into the folds of the self-proclaimed elite and entitled; and in being so envious, serve the self-proclaimed elite and entitled, seeking and proclaiming their ideology, and serving (living according to) their ways.

Don't solve a problem, just make it look like you did something, and you'll get rewarded by those in charge of such things.

So peace prizes are readily handed out to recipients, yet where can mankind find continuous peace and comfort from the tyranny of a system to which they have enslaved themselves?

Philanthropists, beings revered as society's benefactors, continue to endorse those who promote the capitalistic methodology (of operating under monetary incentive/ reward system), in order to keep the wealth flowing from the pockets of others supporting the system; therein taking what rightfully belongs to another, and returning only a portion.

Because you are the offspring of someone who did not understand, nor cares to reason, the natural resources of the world belong equally *to every living entity, past, present, future, you imagine yourself as entitled to take as you please, and give to whomever you please.* There is another name for you besides the one you give yourself. Created in God's image, every man yearns to be a benefactor to someone, even a child; the powerful, entitled, wealthy, and obscenely wealthy take that honor as their own, and so the spirit in man wanes.

Not once does it occur to the self-proclaimed benefactors and business leaders that when they pay far less to another than they give to themselves and those they entitle, and yet charge the same price across the board to everyone no matter how little they have been given, they play favorites to a corrupt and imbalanced system. This from a supposedly advanced intelligent species. There is *no* honor in the monetary incentive/reward system, so too *no* honor in those supporting its ways. And so the spirit in man wanes.

Anger and retaliation abounds as the competition grows heated; suspicions and alienation keep each apart—who will do what, and when will they do it? This person wants what that person has in every institute of man, *and none understand (reason) that what they do is wrong, because everybody is doing it.* It is a polluted, depraved, and destroyed world a child is born into.

And then those who have been cast adrift in the sea of society because they rebel against what they know to be wrong, or they fail to measure up to some standards of a corrupt society, are counseled like they are in the wrong, and conditioned to fall in line. And if those things fail, they are discarded to become prey to the whims and crimes of the depraved and tyrants of society.

What is minimized and called mental illness, for which is prescribed copious amounts of medications and distractions to blot out the confusion and distress created, is nothing more than the soul's inability to deal with the spirit of the guilt of the many deceptions committed. Yet, there is a greater price which will be paid for denial of such, and for those who are ambivalent, and for those who are of two minds.

These are but a few of the ways of fallen men.

The Prosecution's Identification of the Guilty: By the Understanding within This Document, You Are so Named and Numbered

Just as every non-living item or composite has a name to identify the item or composite, every entity identified as having an essence called life has a word which identifies the composite, as in God, Man, Animal, Angelic Being. And as is the nature of man to do so, there are the given names by which one man identifies himself, his children, and others of the species; therefore, the importance of names to God and man is undeniable, and are not names themselves words?

As it was said to "discern the spirits" (see the synonyms for discern) there stands this truth: *man has the ability to discern spirits*, and through the presentation of the statement as a directive, man *has the need* to discern the spirits. Are not spirits as invisible to the eye (as is everything), and yet tangible feelings as in the spirit of love, hate, patriotism, et al. (words); and have you not heard the names lover, hater, patriot—terminology used as a delineator of a particular presence or character trait of an individual?

If the words of the corruption of the world around man are not sufficient evidence of man's corruption before this court, words (or their derivatives) which are spread daily throughout man's communication and entertainment channels, such as: criminal, exploitation, privileged, segregated, raped, murdered, polluted, then there are the words of man's character, which will.

Know this: The Word of God, of the Father of all things, in the spirit of truth, in the beginning, before He separated the waters of the heavens from the waters of the physical dimension, in knowing man, in knowing Satan, and in knowing the nature of all things compromised (sin), chose from the most comprehensive language *being spoken today* to identify the embodiment of the created entity known as Satan, through a selection of words. And from the many possible words, chose six hundred and sixty-six (666) words to be precise, *to capture the essence* of the embodiment.

If any man, woman, or child possesses any number of the compromised attributes, acting, operating, conducting, executing the feelings of the abstract attribute (as being in the spirit of the attribute), that man, woman, and child *is as being numbered along with Satan*; Satan who is the executor of all things compromised, *even if that man, woman, or child, does not possess the full number of 666.*

Satan, and the *compromised* man, woman, and child is so named and numbered by these names and others (and/or their derived or derivatives):

> compromised, belligerent, deceitful, liar, cheat, heinous, jealous, antagonist, deceptive, exploiter, belittling, jeopardizing, slothful, careless, manipulative, ill-tempered, angry, unbeliever, capitalist, rude, haranguing, crude, non-committal, biased,

doubtful, short-sighted, envious, lazy, apathetic, disinterested, faithless, fickle, hoarder, alienator, nagging, quarrelsome, biting, back-stabbing, harsh, objectionable, harping, rapist, hedonist, fornicator, gambler, power-hungry, terrorist, selfish, blindsider, corruptor, perverse, miser, disloyal, bad-mannered, offensive, communist, self-entitled, defensive, unjust, snobbish, bigot, contemptuous, domineering, ambivalent, argumentative, slacker, vain, egotistical, subjugator, morbid, vengeful, obnoxious, presumptive, horrific, irresponsible, procrastinator, agnostic, vexing, objector, bitter, murderer, thief, crooked, cruel, condescending, insipid, insufferable, gratuitous, temperamental, deceitful, philanderer, foul-mouthed, loathsome, filthy, archaic, self-absorbed, caustic, unfair, sanctimonious, inequitable, imbalanced, dreadful, untrustworthy, suspicious, possessive, smug, spoiled, harassing, self-indulgent, corrosive, gruesome, convoluting, criminal, uncooperative, privileged, unmovable, persnickety, vain, abominable, pushy, dreadful, skeptic, sexist, ignorant, masochist, sadist, torturous, underhanded, vile, despicable, lax, debilitating, insincere, ostentatious, arduous, outraged, maligner, loathsome, sick, demented, perverse, guile, evil, crass, compulsive, bewitched, worldly, vindictive, voyeur, negligent, uncaring, passive, atheist, cantankerous, complainer, pretentious, self-indulgent, hypocrite, separatist, halfhearted, carping, et al.

The preceding are only one hundred and sixty-one (161) of the possible six hundred and sixty-six (666) names, any of which may be written upon you even if you possess even the slightest aspect of the quality. Because all are not named here does not mean the ones not named are less important in the judgment of man; it simply means *all mankind is required to discern the spirits of all things evil, and cast every abominable aspect out of yourselves (life).* Seek and you shall find… the rest.

Man presently labors daily to light the fires of desire in his offspring to achieve what he has accomplished: profit for ease, comfort, and entitlement, when it was to have been to labor for love (of) Godly values. And so it is, the buying and selling of any item which was to have been freely given, as God freely gave in the garden, marks a man as numbered along with Satan and all things abominable, and so you are identified as well.

As for those who pervert and diminish the integrity of the union of fleshly gender opposites, substituting excuse for love's true intimacy, nothing more need be said in regard to this matter than the words used here; you are so identified as corrupt as well.

In man's self-righteous self-absorption, this truth has been ignored: it is not how you see yourself in this matter of judgment (reasoning) and how you may minimize a flaw in your character; it is how you are being seen through the perceptions (values) of your judgment—through the spirits of the abstracts which are at the basis of your decisions, such that the world stands as it does today.

You are reasoned (understood, viewed) and judged in the manner of the corruption (words) by which you live, or in the manner of having Godly characteristics or traits (words). When you go to a mirror to view yourself, you should not have been valuing your physical self. Every man, woman, and child has a fleshly exterior and interior consisting of the same words. Those words are not as having value in the Lord making His spiritual disposition (determination) of you.

The essence of *you*, the values which lay beneath the surface of the flesh within the power of reasoning, is more visible when you disregard the alleged values of the flesh which you have never seen to begin with, which you only reasoned for a time to be important. Is this not the understanding of the directives "Discern the spirits" and "Crucify the deeds of the flesh" and have you done this before this moment? And where was it written even once, the flesh (you can't even see with the eyes; only reason) is so important such that it can enter into the heavens?

And do you not become enraptured (caught up) gaining entrance into an ever-increasing understanding and joy of a relationship with God, with every fleshly pursuit being removed (cast out) from value when reasoning? You know these things to be true, yet you deluded yourself and others;

waited and waiting for a physical manifestation of being 'caught up,' which was never promised as coming.

The first death is the act of crucifying the deeds (desires) of (for) the flesh (earthly pursuits) in order that after the second death (which is the death of the flesh), *no evil spirit remain in your word-based spiritual composition*, which if you do have one or any or many of the 666, automatically sends you to the lake of fire. This is what is made new: *Man is renewed as the reasoning creature God created him to be*. No longer is "forgiven" the basis for entering into the Kingdom of God. Man returns to become the reasoning creature he was at the beginning, placing no value to aspects the physical dimension except to simply justly exist in conjunction within the parameters for a time, and for any man to do otherwise, that man, woman, or child goes to the lake of fire.

Was it not said, "Be ye perfect…" is this not what is described in the scripture: "Blessed are those who die in the Lord from now on, for their (perfect) deeds (preceding actions) follow them" and not their compromises?

Having once been forgiven, did not, does not *mean, and will never mean, it is acceptable to live compromised.* But many have lived the lie that somehow it does, and so you cling to your supports which uphold your compromises and sins. And so you continue to suffer, and in doing so cause others to suffer at your hands. So while you may have been issued a covering (robe) in forgiveness, that robe has not remained pure in the sight (reasoning) of God.

The world was not to change; the world stands complete, perfect in its functioning, sustaining and providing for all that dwelled within its word parameters. The flesh of man was the proving ground for what a reasoning creature can do to enhance existence: first, in a dimension other than the heavens, and, ultimately, in the heavens themselves.

There is a point of understanding when mankind realizes what lays at the bottom of the oceans, what lays at the ends of the universe, what lays at the end of time, what lays at the ends of the heavens has no significance compared to what lays within the essence of man himself. Man can equate and attach himself to every possibility, to every element, to every wonder, and be as insignificant as those things are, or be as great as he is.

Clarification of the Sentence of Those Found Responsible in Committing and Perpetuating the Offenses of Mankind

If all were "forgiven" forever, what then is the need for the lake of fire?

Evil and sin is consigned to the lake of fire, and there destroyed. But what is the exact reasoning and interpretation of this determination?

God (invisible to the eye) is a set of specific words reasoned. And (invisible to the eye) man is created in the likeness of those same concepts and principles. In man, reasoning any matter such as abstracts, intuition, imagination, consciousness, reasoning, and memory, it has always been prudent to reason them in the same light God created them in, and to not overlook any of them as in the case of memory which is a highly valued reasoning concept, and an obvious component in the construction of invisible man created in God's invisible image.

One feature of the concept of memory entails (encompasses), reminding oneself of what is truly valuable, like obedience, respect, and honor, peace; and carrying out the actions of those concepts.

Yet, there is another truth to the concept of memory: a person can exist without a particular memory (thought, reasoning). In the matter of God's vengeance (Vengeance is mine…), for man's disregard for the truths of existence, *it* is not *the souls and spirits of disobedient men which will be destroyed from existence*. These men did not (do not) fear God, though they reasoned (know) God exists (as does most men); yet they unceasingly carried out atrocities great and small upon one another. They are spiritual reasoning entities with souls, with their own memories as well, and will experience for all eternity retribution for the misery, corruption, compromises, et al., they have inflicted (reasoned) on others and themselves.

As for those which remain true to God the Father, there is to be destruction of the memory of the lake of fire and all that dwells within it. Recall it was said, "God will wipe away every tear." How does this happen? Understand this clearly: Why should there remain any memory of any soul or spirit who has committed an act of evil; or any lingering memory of any evil committed upon you or anyone else that remains?

The memory of evil, the memory of the souls who committed the evil, and the memory of the pain experienced which the evil have committed, is that which will be destroyed for the benefit of those who were, are, and remain true to the Creator.

As for the evil, they have no such promise of relief. They did not reason this: "The fear of the Lord is (only) the beginning of wisdom." The evil of the world believed the lies of Satan, believing that they could hide their spirits in the darkness of evil, privilege, entitlement, chaos, supposition, conjecture, rhetoric, excuse, lies, and denial. And then when judged and consigned to the lake of fire, when the lake of fire was destroyed, their torment would end and they would have nothing to be concerned about. They would cease to exist.

The Decree of the Prosecution

God did promise an end to the lake of fire and those in it. Fallen man reasoned it in such a way as man, lacking caution and wisdom, would reason it. These men gave no good memories to those they deceived and exploited;

they gave only the ugliness of their selfish desires. And those thoughts are the ones they will have forever as well as knowing in another realm of existence that they have been forgotten. Just as they forgot the needs of others and abandoned them to the tyrants and the depraved of society, so too will they be abandoned to the unspeakable terrors and consequences of those things, those of their own making and those they allowed to be inflicted on others. So too, with this end of evil men, comes the end of Satan.

So be it.

As it is known in the heavens and upon the earth, man is joined to one another in the commonality of the reasoned (spirit of the) words of their existence. What applies to one, applies to all. What is reasoned by one is reasoned by all. The man God created man to be is restored to God.

So be it.

Man *is not* to live, ever again, in the possibilities of what "was" or "will be."

So be it.

Man, children to God and children to one another, knowing what "is," is forever connected to what is, and what is, is the boundary of the understanding of obedience, love, righteousness, peace, and the freedom of these things within the boundaries of Equity.

So be it.

I call now upon the Father, who dwells within every man, woman, and child to execute the reasoning of the words of this document, burning these words into man's consciousness, having this document reproduced and distributed for the purpose of reasoning so long as it is necessary, with the understanding that man *is* aware of his responsibility to God, to the spirit of truth, to God's Word, to the heavens, to one another, to the world.

So be it.

"By all means necessary, establish the peace which surpasses all understanding, in the Heavens and upon the earth, for all eternity."

So be it.

These are the things made new. These are the things which are.

So be it.

There *is* now a specified time allotted, that these things may be so reasoned and come to pass.

So be it.

This concludes the findings, judgment, and decree of the prosecution.

So be it.